MW00387026

Themes to Watch For:

As you read through the book, keep the following 3 questions in mind.

POWER OF SYMBOLS: Watch how certain things become symbolic and swell in meaning. Items that are rather inane become transformed within this impromtu society (conch). Why do these items become so powerful? What sort of things do we have in our society that have this type of power?

LEADERSHIP: Watch how Ralph and Jack lead. Who is more effective? That is, who gets better results? Whose leadership is ultimately better for the boys?

FEAR: What role does fear play in the story? How does Jack use fear to lead? How does Ralph use fear to lead? Do current governments use fear in their leadership? How so?

Ten Essay Questions

1) Towards the end of the story "the chief" and his savages go and steal Piggy's glasses. Why didn't they steal his glasses from the very beginning? What are some of the things that needed to happen before this was viewed as an acceptable act?

2) How is Simon's character, throughout the story, a "Christ-figure"? That is, how is Simon like Christ, both in terms of his character and the things that happen to him?

3) Both Ralph and Simon are "good" characters. Is there a difference in their goodness? What about their goodness is the same?

4) What role do "fear" and "courage" play in the story?

5) Piggy tends to be the most gifted intellectually, and he usually has correct insight as to how they should organize and what they should do. Yet the other boys rarely listen to him and frequently abuse him. Why do you think this is the case? What role does Piggy play in the story? That is, what does piggy add to the story?

6) What is the role that intelligence plays in the story? How do Ralph and Piggy view intelligence and how is this different than how Jack and the hunters view it?

7) What role do the "Littluns" play in the story? What do they represent, analogously, in our society? The older boys treat them in different ways. What does the author reveal about the older boys by how those older boys treat the littluns?

8) How are the forces of civilization and savagery used in the story? Which do you feel the author believes is good? Why?

9) The conch plays a central role in the story. What role does the conch play? How do the boys view the conch at the beginning of the story? How about at the end? What happened to the conch that caused this shift in perspective?

10) The story is about a plane full of boys and the impromtu society that emerges in their crisis. The author intentionally excluded girls from the story as this would add too much complexity to the allegorical nature of the story. How would the story have been different if there were girls on the island with the boys? What conflicts would be added? Would it have made the story better or worse? Why?

Four Learning Activities

1) [for younger students] Draw a map of the island and highlight where all of the major events took place.

2) Design a game (either a board game or a card game) based on the Lord of the Flies. Discuss how the mechanics of the game would work (would there be dice? what would the dice roles signify? etc.). Finally, discuss what the object of the game would be (how would a player know if they had won or not?).

3) Write an epilogue for the book that talks about what happened to the surviving boys when they became adults. What was Ralph like as an adult? Jack? Sam and Eric? Roger?

4) Write a new ending for the story. How else might it have ended? What if there was no Officer and war boat?

UnAnswered Questions

Chapter One: The Sound of the Shell

What is the "long scar smashed into the jungle"? What caused it?

Why do you supposed a person might have a "touch of pride" about having asthma?

Why didn't Ralph ask the fat boy's name?

Why do you suppose Piggy continually refers to "my auntie"?

Does Ralph seem anxious about being on an abandoned island?

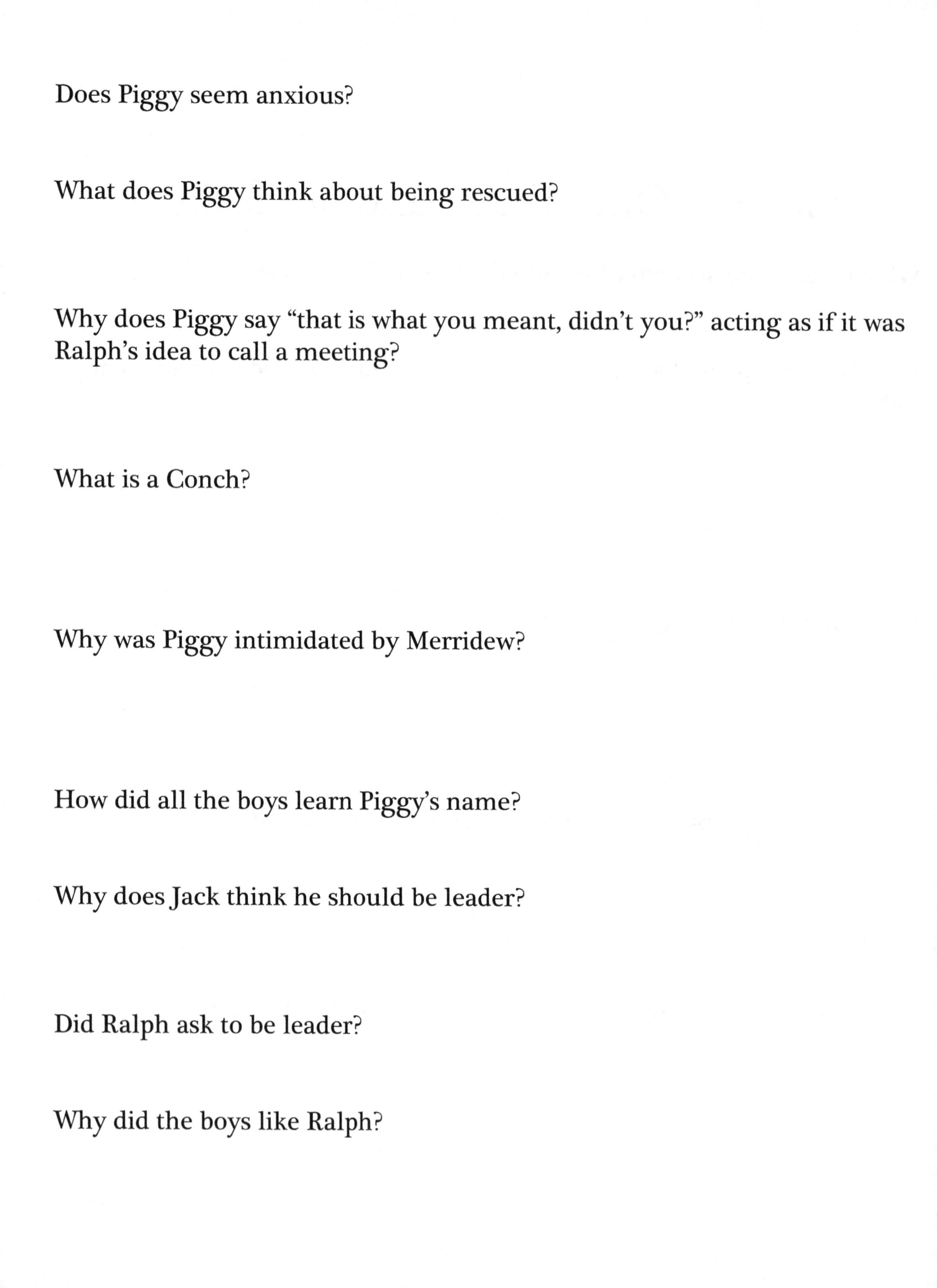

Does Piggy seem anxious?

What does Piggy think about being rescued?

Why does Piggy say “that is what you meant, didn’t you?” acting as if it was Ralph’s idea to call a meeting?

What is a Conch?

Why was Piggy intimidated by Merridew?

How did all the boys learn Piggy’s name?

Why does Jack think he should be leader?

Did Ralph ask to be leader?

Why did the boys like Ralph?

Why was Piggy hesitant to vote for Ralph?

Why might it have been a good idea to "offer something" to Jack?

How did Ralph diffuse Piggy's anger about betraying him by telling everyone his detested nickname?

What did the boys learn by climbing to the top of the mountain?

Did Jack kill the pig?

Chapter Two: Fire on the Mountain

Who is allowed to speak at assemblies?

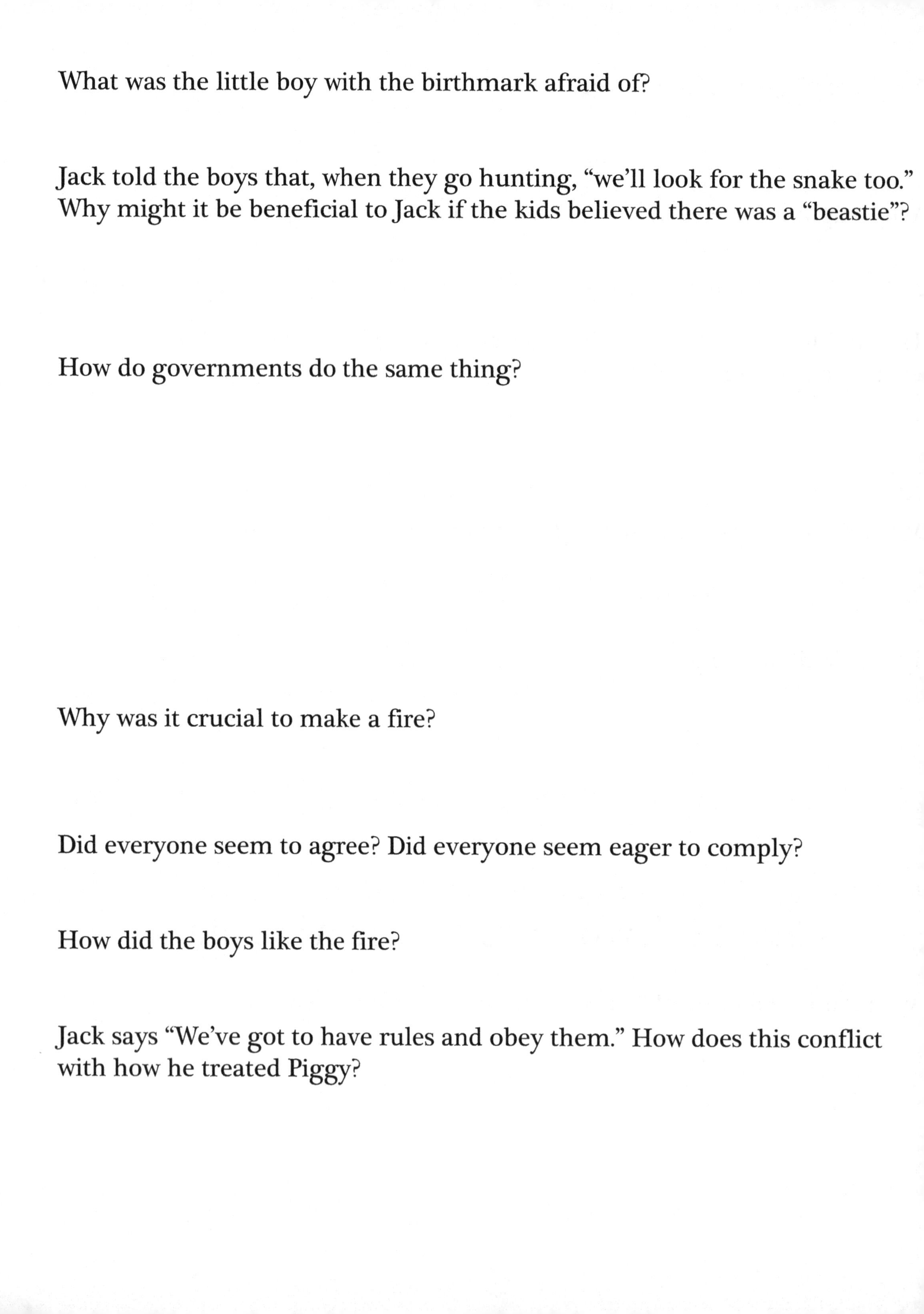

What was the little boy with the birthmark afraid of?

Jack told the boys that, when they go hunting, “we’ll look for the snake too.” Why might it be beneficial to Jack if the kids believed there was a “beastie”?

How do governments do the same thing?

Why was it crucial to make a fire?

Did everyone seem to agree? Did everyone seem eager to comply?

How did the boys like the fire?

Jack says “We’ve got to have rules and obey them.” How does this conflict with how he treated Piggy?

Chapter Three: Huts on the Beach

Does chapter 3 pick up immediately where chapter 2 left off?

Why is Ralph frustrated?

Ralph keeps reminding Jack that Jack hasn't killed anything yet. Why?

How do you think this makes Jack feel?

Does Jack seem to think maintaining a fire is as important as Ralph thinks it is?

How is Ralph's work different than Jack's work?

Chapter Four: Painted Faces and Long Hair

Are the “littluns” thought highly of?

In the paragraph describing the “littluns,” what do you suppose the various sizes of boys represent, metaphorically, about society?

What do you suppose “the transparencies” are?

How did Jack’s painted face make the other boys feel?

What does it mean when Jack, while wearing the painted face, was “liberated from shame and self-consciousness”?

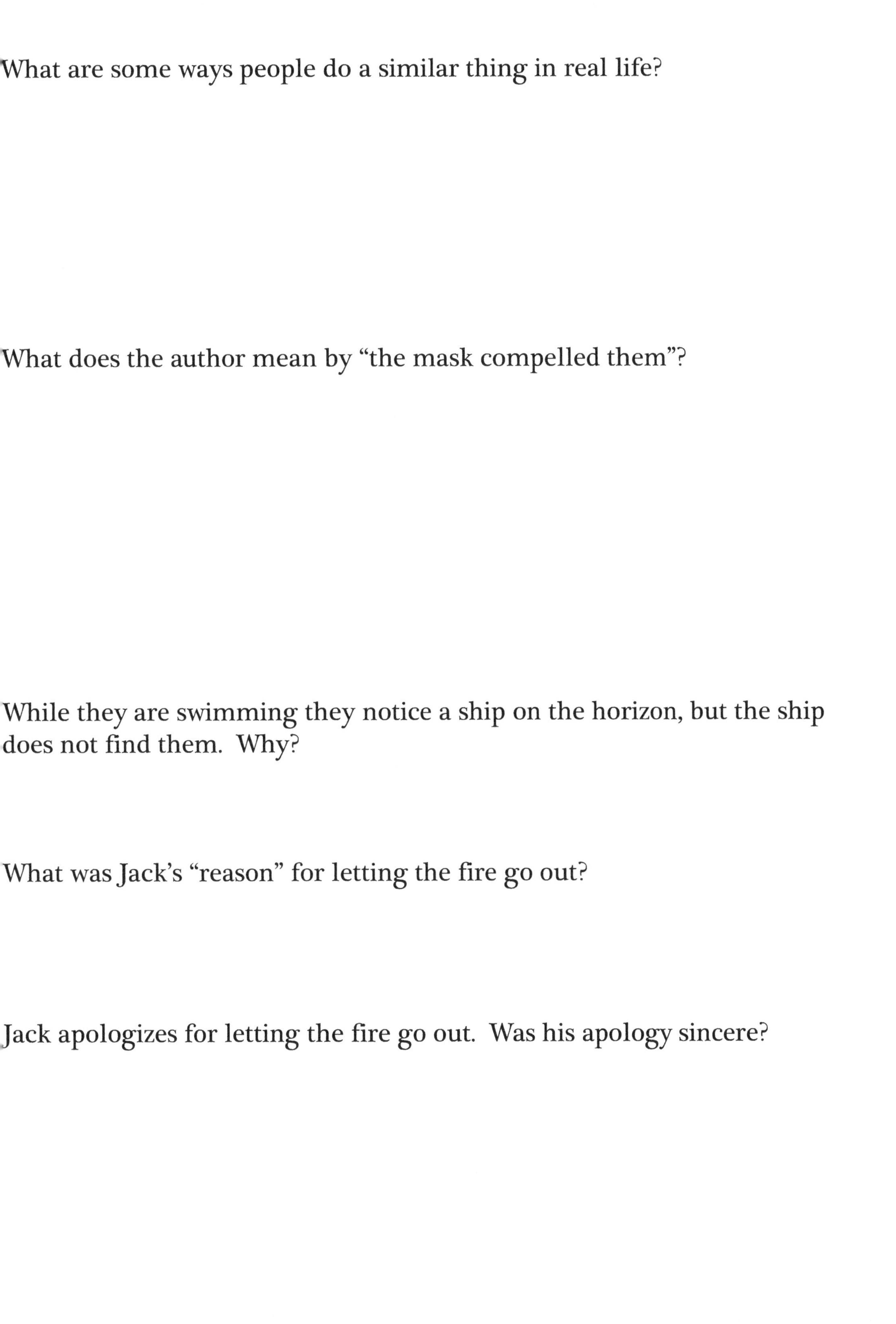

What are some ways people do a similar thing in real life?

What does the author mean by “the mask compelled them”?

While they are swimming they notice a ship on the horizon, but the ship does not find them. Why?

What was Jack’s “reason” for letting the fire go out?

Jack apologizes for letting the fire go out. Was his apology sincere?

After killing the pig, and after the confrontation with Piggy and Ralph, the author says: "Jack was loud and active. He gave orders, sang, whistled..." What is happening to the group? What is happening to Jack?

What does the author mean when he notes: "Jack had meant to leave him in doubt as an assertion of power..."?

The author notes: "Jack looked around for understanding but found only respect." How is respect different than understanding? What did Jack want them to understand? Why is understanding more desirable to Jack? What did they "respect"?

Chapter Five: Beast from the Water

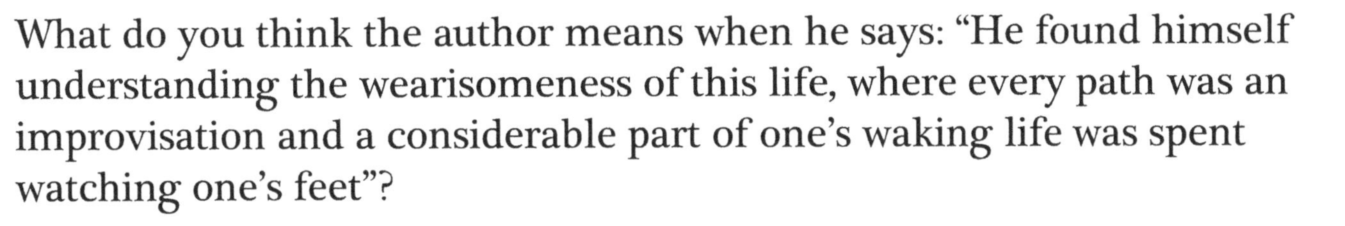

What do you think the author means when he says: "He found himself understanding the wearisomeness of this life, where every path was an improvisation and a considerable part of one's waking life was spent watching one's feet"?

Which "enthusiastic exploration" is Ralph referring to? Why is he remembering it now?

What frustrated Ralph about the "lamentably springy" log?

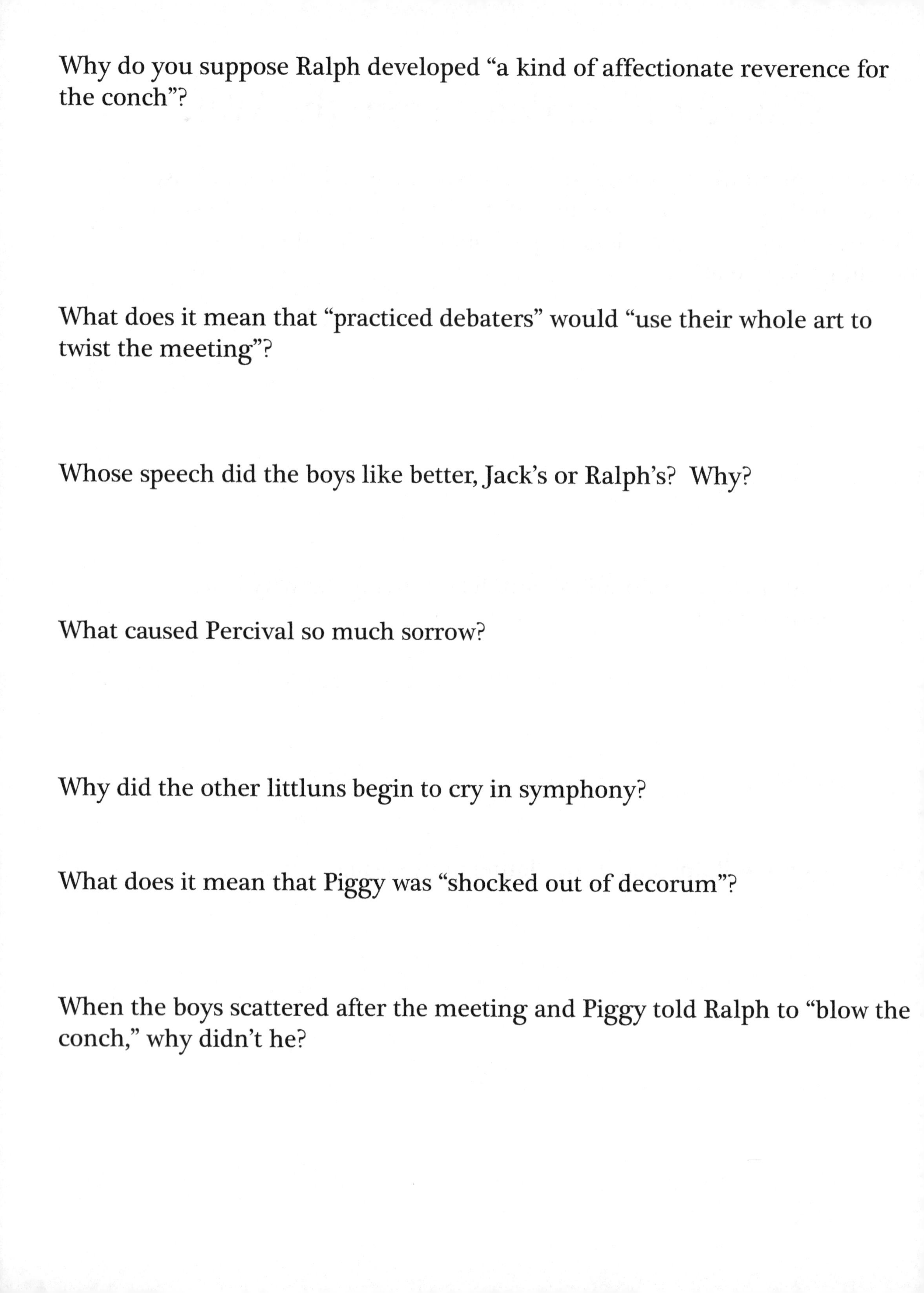

Why do you suppose Ralph developed “a kind of affectionate reverence for the conch”?

What does it mean that “practiced debaters” would “use their whole art to twist the meeting”?

Whose speech did the boys like better, Jack’s or Ralph’s? Why?

What caused Percival so much sorrow?

Why did the other littluns begin to cry in symphony?

What does it mean that Piggy was “shocked out of decorum”?

When the boys scattered after the meeting and Piggy told Ralph to “blow the conch,” why didn’t he?

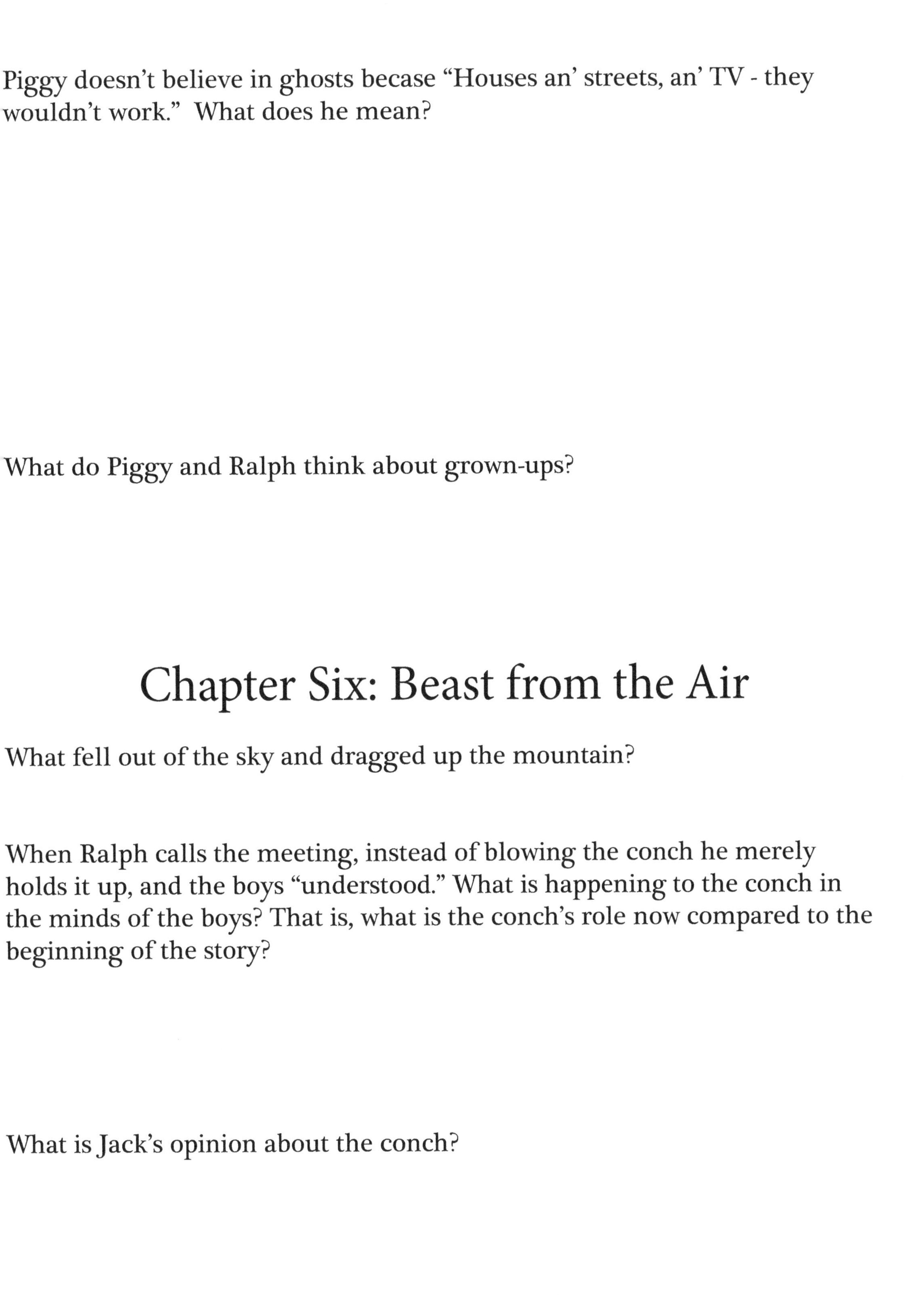

Piggy doesn't believe in ghosts becase "Houses an' streets, an' TV - they wouldn't work." What does he mean?

What do Piggy and Ralph think about grown-ups?

Chapter Six: Beast from the Air

What fell out of the sky and dragged up the mountain?

When Ralph calls the meeting, instead of blowing the conch he merely holds it up, and the boys "understood." What is happening to the conch in the minds of the boys? That is, what is the conch's role now compared to the beginning of the story?

What is Jack's opinion about the conch?

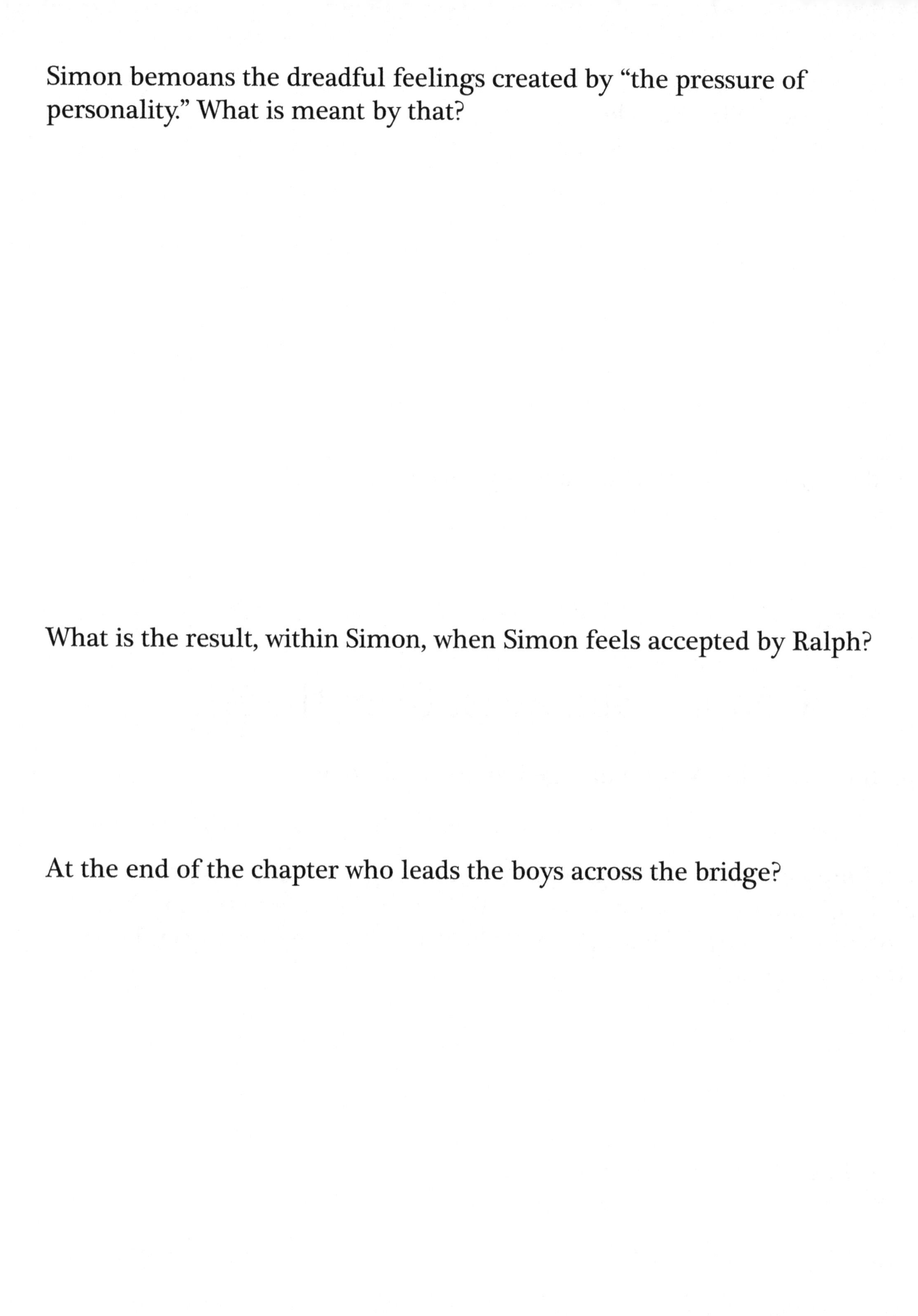
Simon bemoans the dreadful feelings created by “the pressure of personality.” What is meant by that?

What is the result, within Simon, when Simon feels accepted by Ralph?

At the end of the chapter who leads the boys across the bridge?

Chapter Seven: Shadows and Tall Trees

When they surrounded Robert (pretending he was a boar) what went wrong?

How is the "game" they played (with Robert pretending to be the pig) the beginning of a ritual?

As night fell only 3 boys proceeded up the mountain. Who?

Did Ralph "want" to go?

Why did he?

Jack turns to Ralph and Roger saying that he saw something. How does Ralph respond?

Does Jack want to go back up?

Did they see the beast?

What is "the beast" actually?

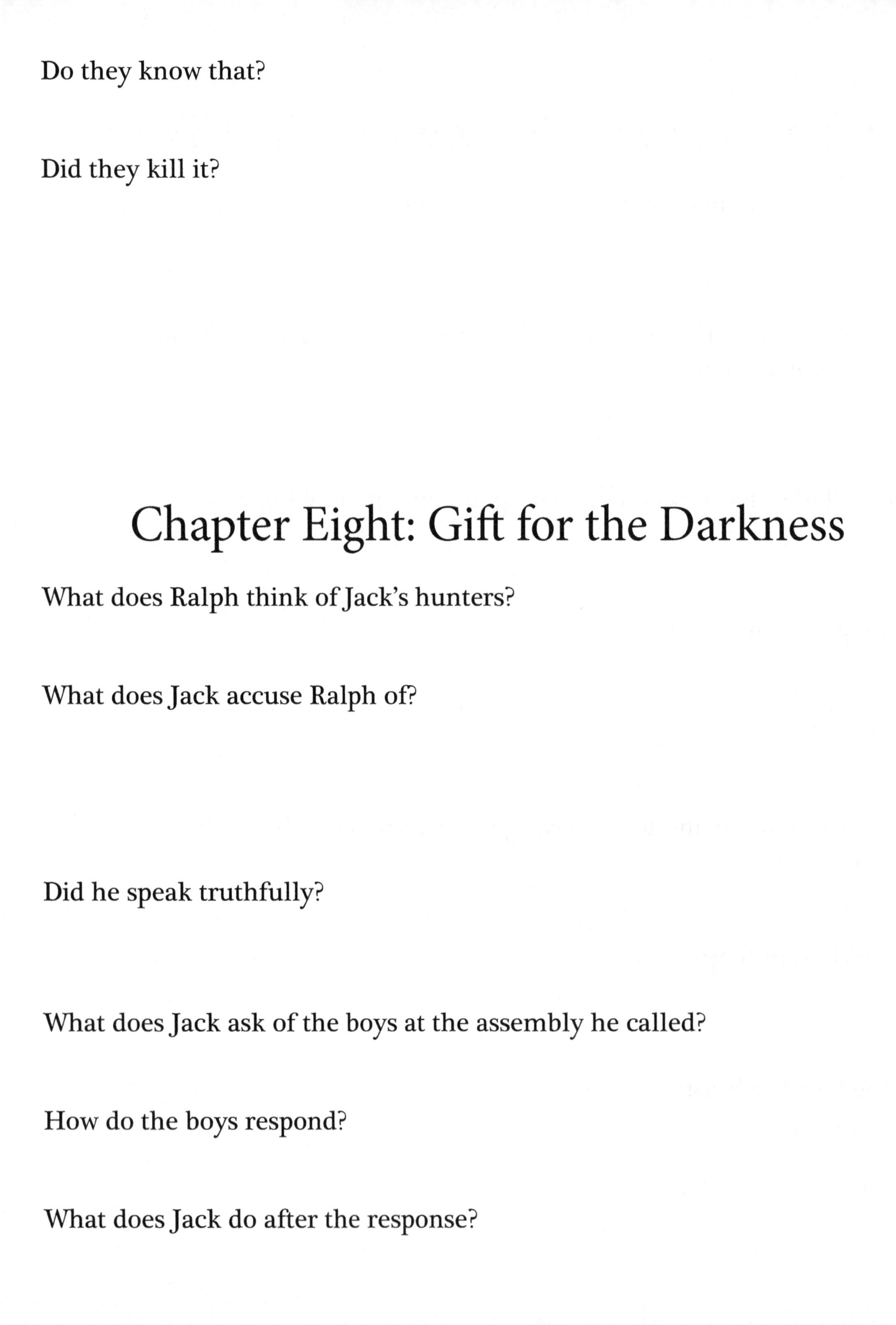

Do they know that?

Did they kill it?

Chapter Eight: Gift for the Darkness

What does Ralph think of Jack's hunters?

What does Jack accuse Ralph of?

Did he speak truthfully?

What does Jack ask of the boys at the assembly he called?

How do the boys respond?

What does Jack do after the response?

What does Simon propose?

How does Piggy feel with Jack being gone?

What is Piggy's proposal as to what they should do next?

When the fire died down what did Ralph and Piggy realize about the remaining boys?

What do the boys think of Simon?

Jack says "We'll hunt. I'm going to be chief." The narrator says "They nodded and the crisis passed easily." What is "the crisis" the narrator refers to?

What is Jack's plan about the beast? He has at least 2 strategies:

What does Jack intend to use to lure boys to his tribe?

After they kill a pig and plan a feast what do Jack and the boys realize they are missing?

What is Jack's solution to this problem?

Who/what is "The lord of the flies"?

Chapter Nine: A View to a Death

Who figures out that the beast is just a deadman with a parachute?

When Ralph and Piggy went to join Jack's party the boys laughed at Piggy, which made everyone feel cheerful and normal. Why do you suppose this is?

As Jack asked the boys to join his tribe Ralph tries to assert his own authority. Does Ralph succeed? Or does Jack?

What is Ralph's argument? What does he threaten to do?

When it started to storm Jack ordered the boys to "Do our dance!" Why?

As they were dancing and chanting, the beast lurched into the party and they killed it. Who did they actually kill?

Chapter Ten: The Shell and the Glasses

How did Piggy try to justify Simon's death?

What does Roger think of Jack as chief?

Why was Roger struck with thoughts of "irresponsible authority"? What is irresponsible authority in this context?

The author stops useing the name "Jack" and uses simply "the chief." Why do you suppose he did this? That is, what is he trying to communicate?

Why might the chief want the boys to continue to believe that the beast is still alive?

The author notes that the chief had a "theological speculation." What does theological mean?

What does this say about the author's use of the beast in the story?

Why did the chief and the hunters attack Ralph and Piggy?

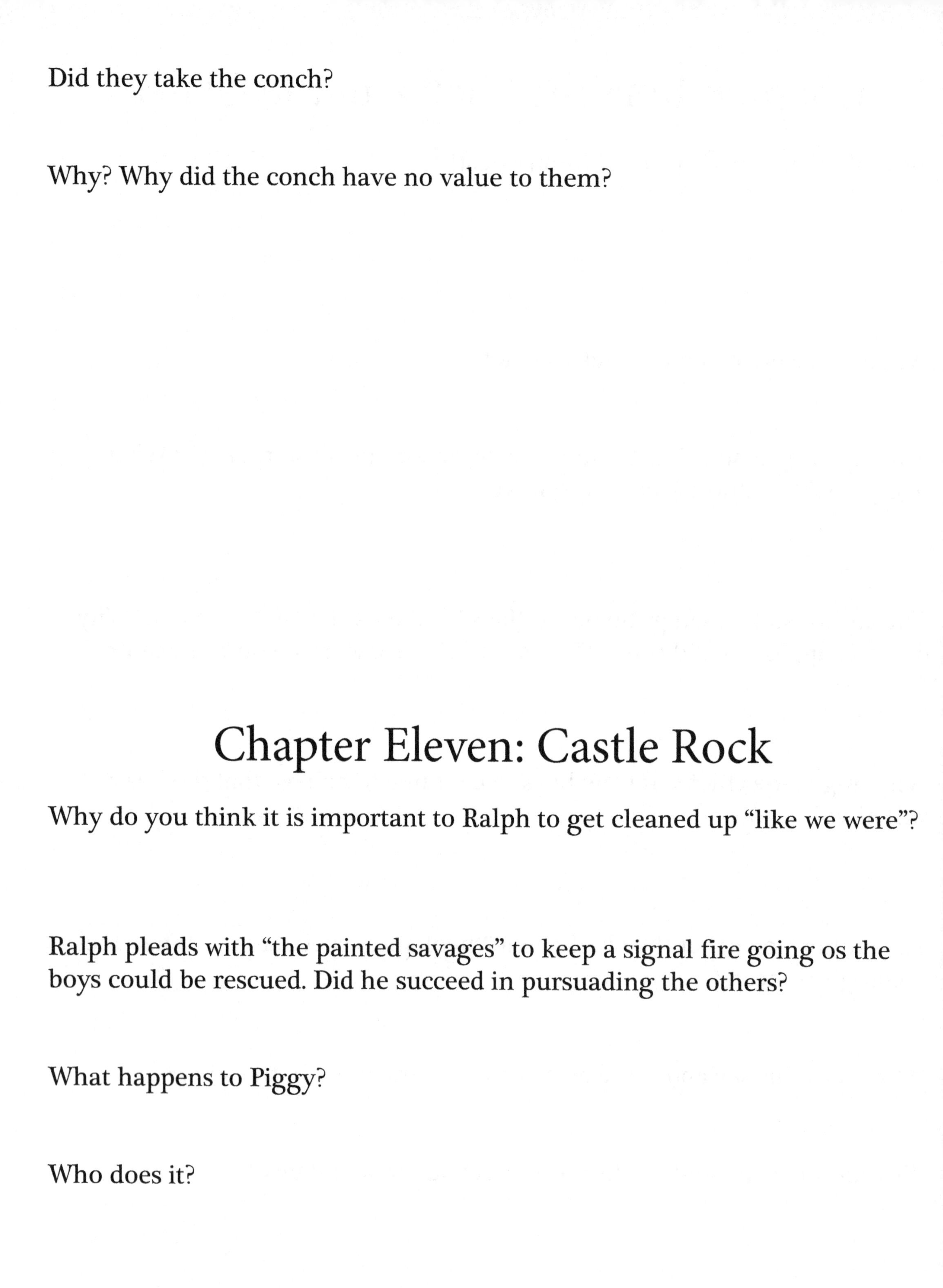

Did they take the conch?

Why? Why did the conch have no value to them?

Chapter Eleven: Castle Rock

Why do you think it is important to Ralph to get cleaned up “like we were”?

Ralph pleads with “the painted savages” to keep a signal fire going os the boys could be rescued. Did he succeed in pursuading the others?

What happens to Piggy?

Who does it?

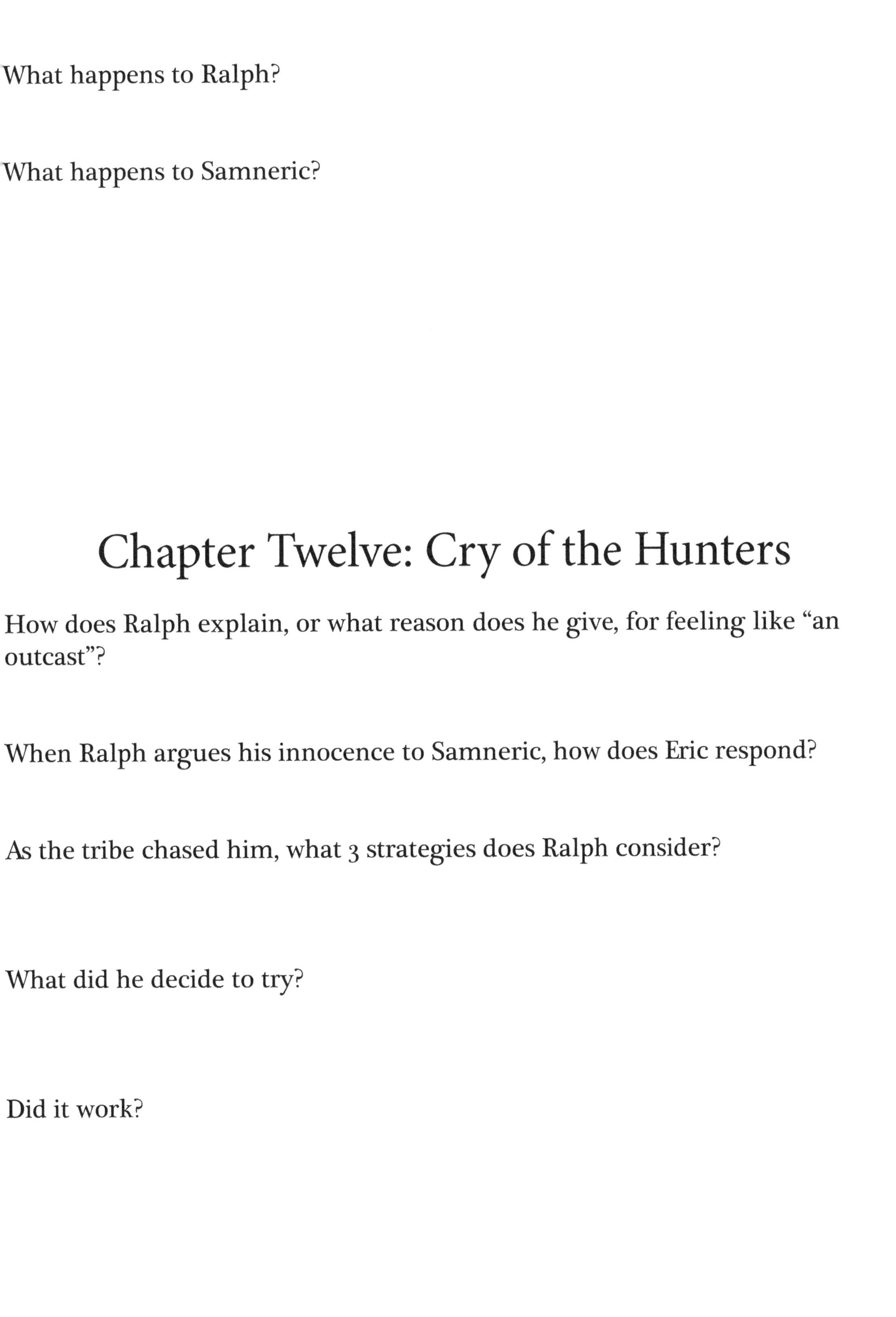

What happens to Ralph?

What happens to Samneric?

Chapter Twelve: Cry of the Hunters

How does Ralph explain, or what reason does he give, for feeling like “an outcast”?

When Ralph argues his innocence to Samneric, how does Eric respond?

As the tribe chased him, what 3 strategies does Ralph consider?

What did he decide to try?

Did it work?

The boys are soon discovered by adults. How? That is, what leads their rescuers to them?

Who finds them and what do you suppose is the author's point in having THESE particular rescuers?

Answers

Chapter One: The Sound of the Shell

What is the "long scar smashed into the jungle"? What caused it?

The "scar" was caused by the plane crashing through the trees.

Why do you supposed a person might have a "touch of pride" about having asthma?

People often wear their shortcomings like a badge. It can be a way of justifying their social limitations (or social status), as if to say "I'm not as socially irrelevant as I seem, it's just that I have this asthma." Having a touch of pride about a limitation can also be a testimony to the obstacles one has had to overcome; a way to amplify the glory of even trivial accomplishments, as if to say "You climbed a mountain? Well I did the same thing with asthma!"

Why didn't Ralph ask the fat boy's name?

Ralph did not care to know the fat boy any better. This is a way the author uses to show that the fat boy was not a socially desirable person. He was sort of a turn off.

Why do you suppose Piggy continually refers to "my auntie"?

Piggy is dependent on authority. He was also most interested in whether there were any adults alive from the crash. Perhaps his dependence on authority stems from his physical limitations ("sucks to your ass-mar!"). More likely, though, his desire for adult presence stems from his social awkwardness and undesireablity. Adults do not necessarily make kids affirm every boy like Piggy, but they do help every boy like Piggy be safe from the hostility of other kids.

Does Ralph seem anxious about being on an abandoned island?

No. Ralph is having fun. Laughing. Swimming.

Does Piggy seem anxious?

Piggy seems especially anxious.

What does Piggy think about being rescued?

Piggy is concerned that everyone else in the world is dead from an atomic bomb.

Why does Piggy say "that is what you meant, didn't you?" acting as if it was Ralph's idea to call a meeting?

Piggy seems insecure in his own ideas. Attributing his idea to Ralph is a way to strengthen the credulity of the idea. It is also, simultaneously, a way to suck up to Ralph; to buy his approval.

What is a Conch?

A conch is a popular tropical sea shell. Technically, it is a "mollusk," which is sort of a shell for slugs (it's actually a PART of the slug that persists even when the slug is gone). The "shell" is a spiral that may bear long projections and have a flared lip. The shape of the shell can amplify sound, especially intense sound blown into one end.

Why was Piggy intimidated by Merridew?

Piggy was intimidated by Merridew's uniform and off-hand authority. Piggy, one who is dependent on authority, experiences dissonance by this apparent authority figure who is a similar age as Piggy.

How did all the boys learn Piggy's name?

Ralph told them.

Why does Jack think he should be leader?

Jack thinks he should be leader because he is a chapter chorister, he is the head boy, and he can sing C-sharp.

Did Ralph ask to be leader?

No.

Why did the boys like Ralph?

There was something appealing about Ralph in the fact that he is the one who called the boys together - in itself, an act of proactive leadership. He was the one who blew the conch. He was also an admirable size for a leader and he had a comforting stillness about him.

Why was Piggy hesitant to vote for Ralph?

Ralph disclosed his nickname to the other boys even though he had asked him not to.

Why might it have been a good idea to "offer something" to Jack?

Ralph could see that Jack wanted to be leader. Offering him an imprtant role would help diffuse the tension of the defeat.

How did Ralph diffuse Piggy's anger about betraying him by telling everyone his detested nickname?

Ralph proposed that his nickname was a better alternative to other names the boys might have called him.

What did the boys learn by climbing to the top of the mountain?

By climbing to the top of the mountain they were able to confirm that they really were on an island.

Chapter Two: Fire on the Mountain

Who is allowed to speak at assemblies?

Whoever is given the conch.

What was the little boy with the birthmark afraid of?

A slithering beast.

Jack told the boys that, when they go hunting, "we'll look for the snake too." Why might it be beneficial to Jack if the kids believed there was a "beastie"?

If the boys are afraid of a beastie, then Jack becomes very important to them, because he has the size and courage to protect them. The more afraid they are, the more important he is.

How do governments do the same thing?

Government, and other organizations, have been accused of trying to make people more afraid of something than is justified with the sole purpose of gaining support (either support for the organization itself, or to support an action the organization wants to take). Citizens, for instance, might now approve of a government attacking a country for their oil; but if that country is supposedly led by an insane dictator who uses chemical weapons, kills innocent people, and eats puppies for breakfast, then citizens may be pursuaded that attacking such a terrible country might be the most ethical action to take.

Why was it crucial to make a fire?

Fire was the only way for them to communicate at a distance. The smoke from the fire was the only thing they could do to be saved.

Did everyone seem to agree? Did everyone seem eager to comply?

Yes. Yes.

How did the boys like the fire?

Piggy's glasses.

Jack says "We've got to have rules and obey them." How does this conflict with how he treated Piggy?

When Piggy had the conch he was supposed to be able to speak, but Jack wouldn't let him. Jack seems to interpret the rules as he needs them.

Chapter Three: Huts on the Beach

Does chapter 3 pick up immediately where chapter 2 left off?

No. Some time has passed, indicated by the author by noting that Jack's hair was now longer.

Why is Ralph frustrated?

The other boys are not helping. They are prone to running off spontaneously. Ralph is trying to get everybody to help build shelters, but even something so central to survival they are failing to help with.

Ralph keeps reminding Jack that Jack hasn't killed anything yet. Why?

Jack is all talk. He talks alot about being a hunter, yet he hasn't actaully killed anything yet. He justifies his lack of assistance with the shelters by claiming to be hunting.

How do you think this makes Jack feel?

Jack probably feels unappreciated and challenged.

Does Jack seem to think maintaining a fire is as important as Ralph thinks it is?

No. "You and your fire!"

How is Ralph's work different than Jack's work?

Ralph is trying to establish basic living conditions and a strategy for getting rescued, which he is not too thrilled to be doing (he'd rather be running around having fun). But Jack LIKES his work (hunting). Jack is doing something that he loves doing. Ralph is doing stuff that is not fun, yet needs to be done.

Chapter Four: Painted Faces and Long Hair

Are the "littluns" thought highly of?

No, they tend to be neglected.

In the paragraph describing the "littluns," what do you suppose the various sizes of boys represent, metaphorically, about society?

One possible answer to this question is that the various sizes of boys represents society's socio-economic strata. The "littluns" represent the poor and powerless.

What do you suppose "the transparencies" are?

Perhaps, Jellyfish.?

How did Jack's painted face make the other boys feel?

Intimidated. Coerced. "The mask compelled them." And, "Bill started up laughing; then suddenly fell silent and blundered away through the bushes." Initially, there was a simple silliness to it, but, discovered by accident, there was a power to it as well. In the same way that Jack could be needed to protect the boys from what they feared, he could now be heeded by being a thing they feared.

What does it mean when Jack, while wearing the painted face, was "liberated from shame and self-consciousness"?

There are multiple ways to interpret this. One way to look at it: In hiding who he really was, and pretending to be someone (something) else, his attention did not have to be pre-occupied with himself. The fact that this made hime feel "liberated" suggests that maybe he was normally insecure/pre-occupied with himself.

Another way to look at it is that, in hiding himself, there was an implicit deniability in his actions. There was a sense in which, by pretending to be someone else, that someone else is responsible for his actions. The masked persona is responsible for the masked persona's actions, not the mask-wearer..

What are some ways people do a similar thing in real life?

There are many possible answers. Job roles ("I was just doing my job"); people running a company might make decisions "in the best interest of the company" that are ethically questionable. They might be inclined to make moral compromises if it benefits share holders. Heck, the corporate structure as a whole has been viewed as a pseudo-identity. Corporations have many rights that an individual has, but is not legally or morally culpable like an individual is.

But people use all sorts of things to mask their real selves and to get what they want. Their wealth, their family name, their status.

What does the author mean by "the mask compelled them"?

The other kids were impressed by the mask, too. They were intimidated by what Jack had become in it. There was a sense in which they allowed Jack + Mask to become something else all together, regardless of the logical incoherence of such a reality. And they understood, intuitively, that this new thing did not have the ethical, or psychological, reservations that Jack as a boy might have.

While they are swimming they notice a ship on the horizon, but the ship does not find them. Why?

The fire is out.

What was Jack's "reason" for letting the fire go out?

He needed everyone for the hunt. "We needed meat."

Jack apologizes for letting the fire go out. Was his apology sincere?

No.

After killing the pig, and after the confrontation with Piggy and Ralph, the author says: "Jack was loud and active. He gave orders, sang, whistled..." What is happening to the group? What is happening to Jack?

Jack is becoming more important, in the boys' eyes, than Ralph. He is pulling the group away.

What does the author mean when he notes: "Jack had meant to leave him in doubt as an assertion of power..."?

Dangling in doubt makes one's dependency obvious. In this case, Piggy's dependency on Jack. The longer that dependency is acknowledged the deeper Jack's power is recognized.

The author notes: "Jack looked around for understanding but found only respect." How is respect different than understanding? What did Jack want them to understand? Why is understanding more desirable to Jack? What did they "respect"?

There are multiple ways to express this. One way: Understanding implies an empathy. Empathy implies solidarity. Jack wanted people to understand his great value and contribution. He wanted to be embraced by the others, affirmed, in a way that recognized this value and contribution. Instead he garnered respect. Respect implies a sort of exultation. Exultation separates: the exulted one is better ("different") than the normal boys. Part of Jack really wanted connection with the other boys. Respect (exultation) created greater separation.

Chapter Five: Beast from the Water

What do you think the author means when he says: "He found himself understanding the wearisomeness of this life, where every path was an improvisation and a considerable part of one's waking life was spent watching one's feet"?

This is an open question with many possible answers. My answer is to look at the what is meant in the statment by 'improvisation' and 'watching one's feet.' By improvisation in this statement I think it means that nothing is given to us. There is no guidance. We have to figure everything out on our own.

The statement 'watching one's feet' refers to the monotonous work required just to sustain and maintain ourselves. It refers to those things that must be done, but don't contribute to growth or advance. It is energy spent, and must be spent, that has no long term return on investment.

Which "enthusiastic exploration" is Ralph referring to? Why is he remembering it now?

Ralph is remembering the initial journey they took up the mountain to determine whether they were on an island or not. He is remembering that exciting journey now because that original journey was drenched in cooperation and respect. But now there was hostility and competition. Ralph is longing for the way things were.

What frustrated Ralph about the "lamentably springy" log?

Nobody took initiative to wedge a rock under it. There was no initiative by any of the boys.

Why do you suppose Ralph developed "a kind of affectionate reverence for the conch"?

Maybe: because it was something that the boys actually respected, and it actually brought the boys together (combatting the tendency towards separation that seemed to be the default reality).

What does it mean that "practiced debaters" would "use their whole art to twist the meeting"?

Other boys, practiced in the art of debate, would be able to use Ralph's meeting for their own agenda.

Whose speech did the boys like better, Jack's or Ralph's? Why?

The boys seemed to prefer Jack's speech over Ralph's. Jack made the boys feel safe. Ralph made the boys feel guilt.

What caused Percival so much sorrow?

He forgot his phone number. His "normal" life, and self, was evaporating.

Why did the other littluns begin to cry in symphony?

They shared in the same sense of loss and evaporation.

What does it mean that Piggy was "shocked out of decorum"?

Piggy was acting shocked because he felt he was "supposed to" be shocked. It is an insincere shock.

When the boys scattered after the meeting and Piggy told Ralph to "blow the conch," why didn't he?

Given the current temperament of the group, he new that if he blew the conch the boys would not respond. Such an act of disobedience would fracture Ralph's authority and set a precedent for disobedience that would ultimately deteriorate Ralph's long term authority.

Piggy doesn't believe in ghosts becase "Houses an' streets, an' TV - they wouldn't work." What does he mean?

Piggy is saying that science has given us tangible results, that the world is predictable and known. The reality of ghosts would conflict with the entire metaphysic (assumption about the world) that led to so much progress. But since we have all of this progress, these assumptions about the world must be true - which means the competing assumption (that there are ghosts) must not be true. Piggy is outlining, in a simplistic way, athe conflict between science and religion; between matter and spirit. Piggy is a budding materialist. Matter is ultimate. Spirit is illusion.

What do Piggy and Ralph think about grown-ups?

Piggy and Ralph seem to idolize them as transcending the tumultous struggles that they are facing. They seem to believe adults have resolved all of the issues that they are facing in their small, impromptu society.

Chapter Six: Beast from the Air

What fell out of the sky and dragged up the mountain?

Parachute pulling a dead pilot.

When Ralph calls the meeting, instead of blowing the conch he merely holds it up, and the boys "understood." What is happening to the conch in the minds of the boys? That is, what is the conch's role now compared to the beginning of the story?

It seems like the conch has become a symbol in and of itself. It used to bring the boys together through the function of blowing. Now it creates response on its own.

What is Jack's opinion about the conch?

Jack feels that the conch is not necessary because it assumes that everyone ought to be able to speak. Jack does not share this assumption. He thinks that some people ought to be able to speak and others ought to know that they shouldn't speak. Some people add value. Others don't.

Simon bemoans the dreadful feelings created by "the pressure of personality." What is meant by that?

There are many ways to articulate what could be meant by this phrase. This is how I would articulate it:

The pressure of personality is the pressure, or anxiety, that results by the confluence of 3 realities: First, we have an innate desire to be affirmed and accepted by others. We desire this event, this act of acceptance, in a core, essential sort of way. But, second, we are dependent on others for this. Being accepted is contingent on the volition, or will, of others. It is, in essence, "up to them" whether we are accepted or not. However, third, even though it we are dependent on others for acceptence, it is still our responsibility, too. We are responsible for creating ourselves; that self that is either accepted or rejected. So the anxiety is amplified by the fact that, even though we are wholly dependent on "others," it is still "our fault" when we are rejected.

What is the result, within Simon, when Simon feels accepted by Ralph?

When Simon feels even the faint sense of acceptance from Ralph (through a faint, sideways smile) he "ceases thinking about himself." Feeling accepted diffuses the "pressure of personality" discussed in the previous question. He feels okay.

At the end of the chapter who leads the boys across the bridge?

Jack is the one who leads the boys across the bridge.

Chapter Seven: Shadows and Tall Trees

When they surrounded Robert (pretending he was a boar) what went wrong?

The boys were playing, but got carried away and became somewhat violent.

How is the "game" they played (with Robert pretending to be the pig) the beginning of a ritual?

Like a ritual, the game involved chanting and exaggerated emotion; then the boys proposed costumes and drums as well.

As night fell only 3 boys proceeded up the mountain. Who?

Ralph, Jack, Roger.

Did Ralph "want" to go?

No.

Why did he?

Jack taunted him into it.

Jack turns to Ralph and Roger saying that he saw something. How does Ralph respond?

Ralph wanted to go see it for himself.

Does Jack want to go back up?

No.

Did they see the beast?

Yes.

What is "the beast" actually?

Dead paratrooper.

Do they know that?

No.

Did they kill it?

No. They fled the mountain

Chapter Eight: Gift for the Darkness

What does Ralph think of Jack's hunters?

Ralph calls Jack's hunters "Boys armed with sticks."

What does Jack accuse Ralph of?

He says that Ralph (1) accused Jack's hunters of being no good (2) is like Piggy (3) is a coward (4) Not a hunter (5) is mysterious - the boys know nothing about him (6) isn't a prefect (7) he just gives orders and expects people to obey for no reason..

Did he speak truthfully?

Jack misrepresented Ralph's comment about the hunters. Also, Ralph didn't just give orders, and people rarely obeyed them when gave them. Otherwise, much of what Jack said was true.

What does Jack ask of the boys at the assembly he called?

Jack asks to vote to dismiss Ralph as leader.

How do the boys respond?

They do not vote against Ralph.

What does Jack do after the response?

What does Simon propose?

Simon proposes to climb the mountain to kill the beast.

How does Piggy feel with Jack being gone?

"more assurance" and a sort of "pleasure." You can imagine that he was relieved to have Jack gone.

What is Piggy's proposal as to what they should do next?

Light a fire; down on the beach.

When the fire died down what did Ralph and Piggy realize about the remaining boys?

Most of the older boys had gone.

What do the boys think of Simon?

He's crazy. "Cracked"!

Jack says "We'll hunt. I'm going to be chief." The narrator says "They nodded and the crisis passed easily." What is "the crisis" the narrator refers to?

The "crisis" was a potential dispute over who would be chief, and/or whether Jack was qualified.

What is Jack's plan about the beast? He has at least 2 strategies:

He has at least 2: (1) "We're going to forget about the beast," and (2) We'll leave a little of each kill for the beast.

What does Jack intend to use to lure boys to his tribe?

Meat.

After they kill a pig and plan a feast what do Jack and the boys realize they are missing?

Fire.

What is Jack's solution to this problem?

Raid the others.

Who/what is "The lord of the flies"?

The sow's head. And, ultimately, death..

Chapter Nine: A View to a Death

Who figures out that the beast is just a deadman with a parachute?

Simon.

When Ralph and Piggy went to join Jack's party the boys laughed at Piggy, which made everyone feel cheerful and normal. Why do you suppose this is?

I suppose this is because having a common enemy unites those in opposition to that enemy, even if those who are in opposition have their own conflicts between themselves.

As Jack asked the boys to join his tribe Ralph tries to assert his own authority. Does Ralph succeed? Or does Jack?

Jack succeeds.

What is Ralph's argument? What does he threaten to do?

Ralph argues that he is still chief because "you chose me." He then argues that Jack is not a leader, but mearly a hunter. And, finally, he argues that he is the leader because he has the conch. He then threatens to blow the conch and call an assembly.

When it started to storm Jack ordered the boys to "Do our dance!" Why?

The littluns were getting scared and even the hunters were getting uneasy. The chanting and dance became a steady pulse, a single organism, that made the boys feel more powerful as they became more and more a part of the dance.

As they were dancing and chanting, the beast lurched into the party and they killed it. Who did they actually kill?

Chapter Ten: The Shell and the Glasses

How did Piggy try to justify Simon's death?

He blamed circumstance (it was dark, the bloody dance, there was the storm, and they were scared). Denial (perhaps he is still alive). It was an accident (they did not intend to kill him). Blamed the victim (Simon shouldn't crawl like that in the dark, he was batty, he asked for it).

What does Roger think of Jack as chief?

"He's a proper chief, isn't he?"

Why was Roger struck with thoughts of "irresponsible authority"? What is irresponsible authority in this context?

Because the chief was going to punish Wilfred without giving a reason why.

The author stops useing the name "Jack" and uses simply "the chief." Why do you suppose he did this? That is, what is he trying to communicate?

The chief is, like the mask, a persona. Jack, the boy, has diminished progressively and is at this point almost gone.

Why might the chief want the boys to continue to believe that the beast is still alive?

Like before, it adds value to Jack as leader, as he can protect the boys from the beast.

The author notes that the chief had a "theological speculation." What does theological mean?

Theological means to study God, or the supernateral.

What does this say about the author's use of the beast in the story?

The beast, in it's unverifiablity and on it's loose evidence, becomes an analogy of religion and religious narratives..

Why did the chief and the hunters attack Ralph and Piggy?

To get Piggy's glasses.

Did they take the conch?

No.

Why? Why did the conch have no value to them?

The conch was an instrument of democracy, where everyone had a right to speak. The new civilization was an autocracy. Only the chief had a right to speak. The conch was unnecessary.

Chapter Eleven: Castle Rock

Why do you think it is important to Ralph to get cleaned up "like we were"?

There are various answers, like: they wanted to regain their dignity. They wanted to be percieved as being more competent. They wanted to be percieved as being civilized, and to contrast the others' decent into savagery.

Ralph pleads with "the painted savages" to keep a signal fire going os the boys could be rescued. Did he succeed in pursuading the others?

No. They mostly laughed.

What happens to Piggy?

Piggy gets crushed by the boulder, knocked to the rocks.

Who does it?

Roger. The boy who was "struck with thoughts of irresponsible authority."

What happens to Ralph?

Ralph flees.

What happens to Samneric?

They were forced to join the tribe.

Chapter Twelve: Cry of the Hunters

How does Ralph explain, or what reason does he give, for feeling like "an outcast"?

"'Cos I had some sense."

When Ralph argues his innocence to Samneric, how does Eric respond?

"Nevermind what's sense. That's gone."

As the tribe chased him, what 3 strategies does Ralph consider?

He could either (1) break through the search line, (2) climb a tree, (3) hide till the boys pass.

What did he decide to try?

Ralph tried to hide.

Did it work?

No. He was found.

The boys are soon discovered by adults. How? That is, what leads their rescuers to them?

A boat full of men found them because they saw the smoke from the forest fire, confirming Ralph's leadership and perspective.

Who finds them and what do you suppose is the author's point in having THESE particular rescuers?

The boys were discovered by an officer of a military cruiser. With this the author makes the salient point that the horrors of the island, born of boys, are the same horrors in the real world, born of adults.

Conclusion

Please go to thatDanKent.com for more study guides, study guide answers, great articles, and funny cartoons.

Also, please follow @thatdankent on Twitter.

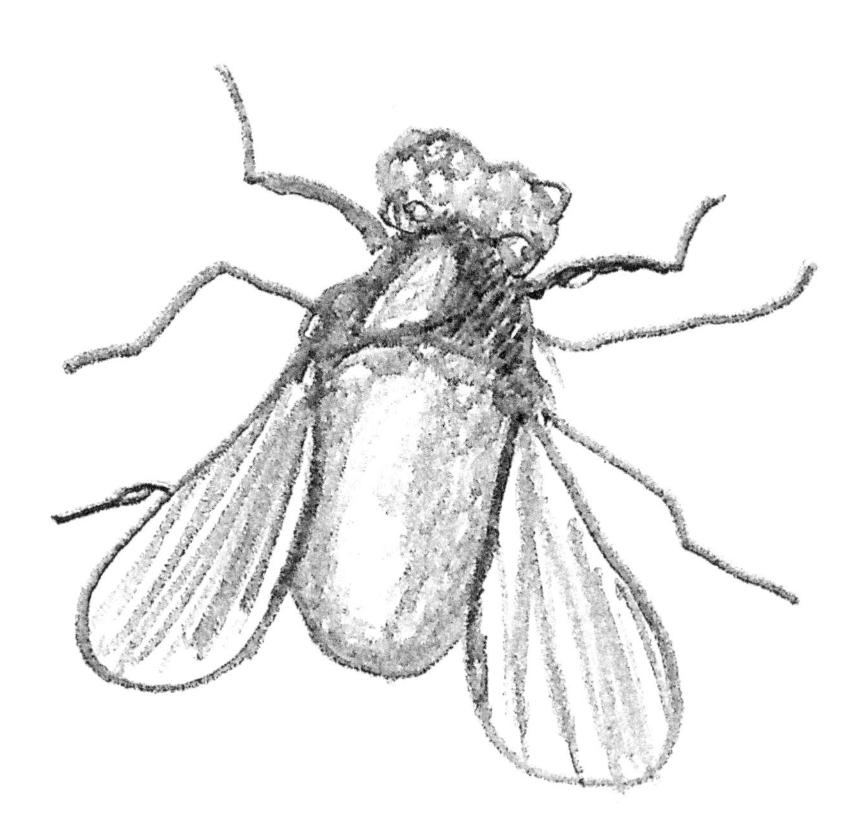

Made in the USA
Las Vegas, NV
04 November 2020